Frontispiece: The Coronation procession of Edward VI leaving the Tower in 1547

British Museum

DEPARTMENT OF THE ENVIRONMENT

THE TOWER OF LONDON

LONDON
HER MAJESTY'S STATIONERY OFFICE

Crown Copyright 1974
First Published 1953
Fifth Edition 1974
Third Impression 1980

ISBN 0 11 670326 1

THE TOWER OF LONDON was first built by William the Conqueror, for the purpose of protecting and controlling the city. As first planned, it lay within the Roman city walls, but its enlargement in the thirteenth century carried its boundaries eastwards beyond the walls. Nowadays it is wholly within the borough of Tower Hamlets. Including the moat, it covers an area of 18 acres (7.3ha).

Of the present buildings only the White Tower is of the Norman period; but architecture of almost all the styles which have flourished in England may be found within the walls. The Tower has in the past been a fortress, a palace and a prison, and has housed the Royal Mint, the Public Records and (for a short time) the Royal Observatory. It was for centuries the arsenal for small arms and, being one of the strongest fortresses in the land, the Tower has from early times guarded the Crown Jewels. From the thirteenth century until 1834 it also housed the Royal Menagerie, the predecessor of the London Zoo.

The oldest and most important building is the Great Tower or Keep, called the White Tower. The Inner Ward is defended by a wall containing thirteen towers, the only surviving original entrance to it being that on the south side under the Bloody Tower. The Outer Ward is defended by a second wall, flanked by six towers on the river face, and by two semicircular bastions at the north-west and north-east. A Ditch or Moat, now dry, encircles the whole; it is crossed at the south-western angle by a stone bridge, formerly the drawbridge, leading to the Byward Tower from the Middle Tower, where there was another drawbridge. In front of this was an outwork called the Lion Tower, also surrounded by a moat, which was crossed by a stone causeway, exposed to view in 1936–37. This causeway included a third drawbridge.

The Tower was occupied as a palace by all our Kings and Queens down to James I. It was the custom for each monarch to lodge in the Tower before his coronation, and to ride in procession to Westminster through the city. The Palace buildings stood between the White Tower and the Inner Wall eastward of the Bloody Tower.

Throughout its history the Tower has also been used as the principal place of confinement for State prisoners, from Ralf Flambard in the early twelfth century to Roger Casement (April–May, 1916) and Hitler's deputy, Rudolf Hess (May, 1941), in the twentieth, as well as other historic personages named in later paragraphs of this guide.

TOWER HILL

The best general view of the Tower is obtained from the gardens to the east of All Hallows Church or from the top of Tower Hill. (To reach the Tower from the underground railway station, however, the visitor should make use of the pedestrian crossing.) In the railed space of Trinity Square, at the top of Tower Hill, the first permanent scaffold on Tower Hill was set up in the reign of Edward IV in 1465, but the first execution recorded here was that of Sir Simon Burley in 1388. Here also were beheaded, among others, Dudley, the minister of Henry VII (1510), his son the Duke of Northumberland (1553), his grandson Lord Guildford Dudley (1554), More and Fisher (1535), Thomas Cromwell, Earl of Essex (1540), Surrey (1547) and his son Norfolk (1572), Strafford (1641) and Archbishop Laud (1645), and the Scottish Lords in 1716, 1746, and 1747, the last being Simon, Lord Lovat.

Passing down the west side of the Tower, one sees the Tower Moat. It was drained in 1843. On January 7th, 1928, at 1.30 a.m., a very high tide swept over the wharf, destroying portions of the retaining walls of the Moat, filling it completely and flooding the Byward Tower to a depth of 4ft (1.2m). As we approach the entrance, we have a good view of the fortifications. On the left is Legge's Mount. To the right is the entrance gateway. The highest building behind is the White Tower, easily distinguished by its four turrets. In front of it are the Devereux, Beauchamp, and Bell Towers, the residence of the Governor being in the gabled and timber-framed house between the last two.

Queen Elizabeth I, before her accession, was imprisoned in the Tower by her sister Mary, on suspicion of being implicated in Wyat's Protestant rebellion. She is said to have used this part of the walls for exercise, and to this day the ramparts between the Beauchamp Tower and the Bell Tower are known as Elizabeth's Walk.

The Tower of London, from an engraving by Wenceslaus Holler

The Tower from an engraving based on a survey of 1597

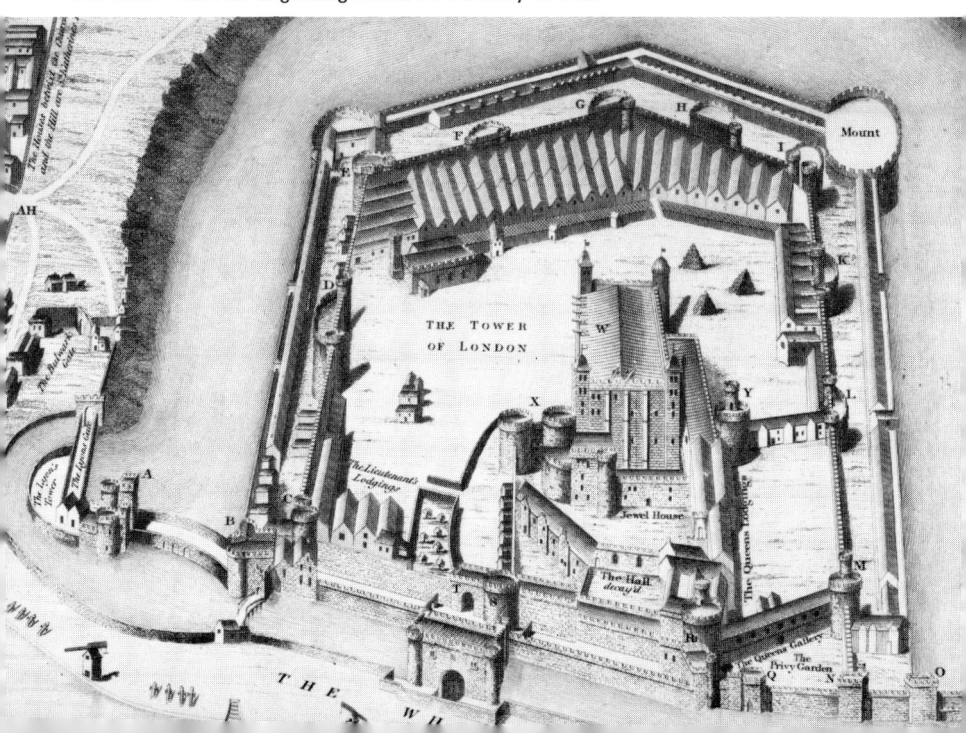

THE ENTRANCE

The modern entrance to the Tower, completed in 1966, passes over the stone causeway which was the only way into the Tower by land in the Middle Ages. This causeway was built by Edward I (1278) and crossed the Outer Moat to the Lion Tower. It had a drawbridge at its outer end, where stood the Lion Gate, and the pit of this drawbridge and the curved slots for its counterweights should be noticed. The Outer Moat was filled up in the latter part of the seventeenth century, and the causeway was buried. It was rediscovered in 1936, and is now exposed to view.

THE LION TOWER

The Lion Tower was a wide semicircle, which stood where the bookshop and refreshment room are now. Part of the line of curved outer wall is marked in the roadway. From the thirteenth century to 1834 the Royal Menagerie was lodged within and near it. Another short causeway, still buried on its south side, leads to

THE MIDDLE TOWER

This also was originally built by Edward I, but it was largely rebuilt in the early eighteenth century. In front of it was the second drawbridge, and the arch under the north side of the causeway let water from the Inner Moat into the drawbridge pit, which exists under the road. Beyond the Middle Tower is the Inner Moat, crossed by another causeway where there was a third drawbridge.

THE BYWARD TOWER

This gatehouse of the Outer Ward is the main entrance through the outer circuit of walls. It was built at the end of the thirteenth century, with additions of the time of Richard II. The timber superstructure on the inside was rebuilt in the early sixteenth century. The portcullis with the machinery for raising and lowering it can be seen on the first floor. On either side of the archway are guardrooms with vaulted stone roofs and hooded fireplaces. Part of a fourteenth-century wall-painting, which includes the figures of St John the Baptist and St Michael depicted against a background

The Byward Tower

decorated with the leopards of England and fleurs-de-lis of France, has been uncovered in the principal room over the gate passage.

THE BELL TOWER

This was planned probably in the reign of Richard I, though its earliest details point to a date early in the thirteenth century. Here Fisher, Bishop of Rochester, Sir Thomas More, the Princess Elizabeth, and James, Duke of Monmouth, were confined. The Curtain Wall east of this tower is pierced by the windows of the Lieutenant's Lodgings, now called the Queen's House, and one of these windows lights the Council Chamber, where Guy Fawkes and his fellow conspirators were examined by the Council in 1605 before their public trial at Westminster

The Traitors' Gate beneath St Thomas's Tower

THE TRAITORS' GATE

On the right is now St Thomas's Tower, with the Traitors' Gate beneath: the wide span of the arch should be noticed. This gate, when the Thames was more of a highway than it is at present, was often used as an entrance to the Tower. In later times it was found convenient as a landing-place for prisoners who had been tried at Westminster. Here successively Edward, Duke of Buckingham (1521), Sir Thomas More, Queen Anne Boleyn (1536), Thomas Cromwell, Earl of Essex, Queen Katharine Howard (1542), Edward Seymour, Duke of Somerset (1551), the Princess Elizabeth, Robert Devereux, Earl of Essex (1601), and James, Duke of Monmouth (1685), passed under the arch on their way to prison or the scaffold. St Thomas's Tower was built by Edward I, and contains a small chapel or oratory dedicated to St Thomas of Canterbury.

The portcullis mechanism in the Bloody Tower

THE BLOODY TOWER

The gateway was built by Henry III and the tower was added over it in the reign of Richard II. It was known by its present name by 1597, possibly from the suicide there in 1585 of Henry Percy, 8th Earl of Northumberland. It is also by tradition the scene of the murder in 1483 of the boy princes, Edward V and his brother, the Duke of York. It was originally known as the Garden Tower, as it gives upon that part of the open space which was formerly the Constable's garden. Here Sir Walter Ralegh, whose portrait hangs over the fireplace, was allowed to walk at one time during the twelve years' imprisonment that followed the abortive attempt, at the end of 1603, to place James I's crown on the head of Lady Arabella Stuart. Most of that time Ralegh was detained in the Bloody Tower. His rooms, we are told, were not uncomfortably furnished, his wife and son could visit him, and he had two servants.

The Bloody Tower (left) and the Wakefield Tower

In 1616 the King released Ralegh for a fresh expedition to the West Indies; but although he was no doubt hoping for the lion's share of the spoils, James also warned the Spaniards. Continual disaster overtook the expedition, and in August, 1618, Ralegh was once again lodged in the Tower. This time, the King meant to be rid of him. And, on the ground that Ralegh's former sentence still held good, he was beheaded on October 29th in Old Palace Yard, Westminster.

Other prominent occupants of this tower were Laud, Judge Jeffreys, Cranmer, Ridley and Latimer.

Immediately joining this tower on the east is

THE WAKEFIELD TOWER

The work now to be seen points to its having been built by Henry III. The Great Hall, memorable as the scene of Anne Boleyn's trial, adjoined it, but was pulled down during the Commonwealth. In 1360 the records of the kingdom, which had previously been kept in the White Tower, were lodged here, and this is called in ancient surveys sometimes the Record Tower, sometimes the Hall Tower. The present name is probably derived from William de Wakefield, King's Clerk, appointed to hold custody of the Exchanges in the Tower in 1344. The Tower has two floors; the ground floor acted as a guard room to the thirteenth-century postern which once led to the Royal Apartments. The remains of this small water-gate, which lay immediately against the east side of the Wakefield Tower and a part of Henry III's curtain running eastwards, were revealed in 1957. The upper floor of the Wakefield Tower contains a single vaulted chamber of some magnificence. Under Edward I, a bridge gave access from St Thomas's Tower to the Palace via the doorway in the south side of this chamber. The present bridge is a nineteenth-century reconstruction, but the original doorways at either end survive.

Henry VI, the last King of the House of Lancaster, was found dead, believed murdered, in 1471 in the Oratory opening off the east of the chamber.

HISTORY GALLERY

East of the Wakefield Tower and approached through an arch in the curtain wall is the History Gallery, opened in 1978 to commemorate the 900th anniversary of the White Tower. Panel displays trace the story of the Tower of London in words and pictures, and set out the Tower's architectural development. Models of the Tower of London in 1547 and 1866 are included.

THE WALL OF THE INMOST WARD

Running north from the Wakefield Tower is a length of wall built by Henry III. This formed part of the western side of the Inmost Ward, and is pierced

The Royal Mint within the Tower in the 18th century

The Royal Menagerie in the Lion Tower in 1779

with loopholes, each loophole being in an arched recess on the inner or eastern face of the wall. At its north end it terminated level with the White Tower, and at this point was situated the Coldharbour Tower, which was the main gateway into the Inmost Ward, and is now destroyed. The foundations of the rounded fronts of its two towers have recently been exposed. This length of wall and the foundations of the gateway-towers were for long embedded in a modern building known as the Main Guard. This was destroyed by enemy bombs on December 29th, 1940, and the medieval wall has been carefully cleared of the ruins.

THE CROWN JEWELS

Most of the magnificent regalia displayed date from the seventeenth century. Nearly all the regalia of six centuries of the English monarchy were sold or melted down by Oliver Cromwell. At the Restoration of the monarchy in 1660 as much as possible was recovered and new regalia were made resembling the old.

The Crown Jewels are now displayed in the Upper and Lower Chambers of the Jewel House. A full description is given in the official guide to the Crown Jewels.

Crowns. The earliest Sovereign's Crown now extant is the lineal successor of King Edward the Confessor's crown (hence its name St Edward's Crown), and was made for the coronation of Charles II.

The earliest Queen's Crown was made for Mary of Modena, consort of James II.

The Imperial State Crown with two arches was made for the coronation of Queen Victoria in 1838. In it is set one ancient jewel, the balas ruby said to have been given to the Black Prince by Pedro the Cruel after the battle of Najara, 1367, and later worn by Henry V in the coronet surrounding his helmet at the battle of Agincourt, 1415. The crown later had added to it the second largest of 'The Stars of Africa', cut from the Cullinan diamond, and altogether contains over 3000 precious stones, mainly diamonds and pearls.

Set in the crown made in 1937 for the coronation of Queen Elizabeth the Queen Mother is the famous Indian diamond known as the Koh-i-noor.

Orbs. The larger Orb was made for Charles II, the smaller for Mary II, consort of William III.

Sceptres. St Edward's Staff, of gold, 4ft 7in (1.4m) long, is surmounted by an orb. The original was supposed to contain a fragment of the True Cross.

The Imperial State Crown

The Royal Sceptre, surmounted by a cross, contains the largest of 'The Stars of Africa', cut from the Cullinan diamond. This is the biggest cut diamond in the world, weighing 530 carats.

The Sceptre with the dove is delivered into the Sovereign's left hand at the coronation.

The Queen's Sceptre with the cross was made for Mary of Modena.

The Queen's Sceptre with the dove was made for Mary II.

The Queen's ivory Rod, mounted in gold and enamelled, was also made for Mary of Modena.

Other Regalia. The pair of gold and enamelled Bracelets were made for Charles II, but were never used. The gold Armills which have replaced them were used at the coronation of Queen Elizabeth II.

The Gold Spurs of St George were formerly buckled on as the emblems of chivalry. They are now touched by the Sovereign and placed on the altar.

The Romanesque Anointing-spoon is one of the two ancient pieces which survive. It dates from the end of the twelfth century and was perhaps made for the coronation of John (1199–1216). The bowl of the spoon was restored for Charles II.

The ampulla, the vessel in the form of an eagle, which contains the oil for the anointing, is the other ancient piece, though not so old as the spoon. It dates in all probability from the time of Henry IV (1399–1413), but was restored for Charles II.

Left: The Sovereign's Orb
Below left: The Ampulla and Spoon
Below right: The State Salt

Plate. Besides the regalia proper, much royal plate is displayed, both ecclesiastical and secular. Some pieces have been used at coronations and other State occasions in the past; others are still so used. One fine piece of plate, 'Queen Elizabeth's Salt' dates from 1572-73 : the remainder is practically all of the time of Charles II or William and Mary II.

The Swords of State include the *Curtana* (without a point) denoting Mercy and the State Sword used at the opening of Parliament. Maces and trumpets are also displayed, some of them used at earlier coronations, and in other cases are the insignia of the Orders of Knighthood, with their collars, stars and badges, and the highest of all decorations for valour, the Victoria Cross and the George Cross.

THE EARLIEST FORTRESS

The Conqueror, before he entered London, ordered the construction of an advanced command post and, after his coronation at Christmas 1066, withdrew to Barking while the works were completed. The defended area was quite small, the south and east sides being formed by the river and the Roman city wall (repaired by King Alfred in 885), and the north and west sides by a newly dug ditch and rampart marked by the wall of the Inmost Ward. This wall was built within the early garrison-fort, the supervision of the work being entrusted to Gundulf, a monk of Bec in Normandy who later became Bishop of Rochester. In 1097, under William Rufus, the works were still going on. A great storm in 1091 damaged the outworks. Ralf Flambard, Bishop of Durham, who was imprisoned in the Keep by Henry I, contrived to escape in 1101. During the wars between Stephen and Matilda, the Earl of Essex was Constable of the Tower, and even obtained a grant of the City of London. When he fell into Stephen's hands, the Tower formed the ransom, and the citizens regained their ancient Liberty. When Richard I was absent on the Crusade, his regent, Longchamp, resided in the Tower, of which he greatly enlarged the precincts by trespasses on the land of the City and of St Katherine's Hospital. He surrendered the Tower to the citizens, led by Prince John, in 1191.

The whole Tower was held in pledge for the completion of Magna Carta in 1215 and 1216. At this time the Roman city wall and the river still formed the east and south side of the castle, but a new ditch was dug and curtain wall built, extending to the defended area to the west. The new defences ran from the Roman city wall just north of the White Tower, across what is now the Broad Walk to the site of the later Beauchamp Tower. From

The White Tower

The Tower and Tower Bridge from the
Port of London Authority building

The view from Tower Bridge

there they turned southward to the river. The Bell Tower and the curtain wall between it and the Bloody Tower are all that survive of the defences of this time.

THE WHITE TOWER OR KEEP

The White Tower, commenced by the Conqueror and completed by William Rufus, is the oldest visible part of the fortress and is one of the earliest and largest keeps in Western Europe. In plan it is somewhat irregular for although it looks so square from the river its four sides are all of different lengths, and three of its corners are not right-angles. The west side is 107ft (32.6m) from north to south. The south side measures 118ft (35.9m). It has four turrets at the corners, three of them square, the fourth, that on the north-east, being circular. From floor to battlements it is 90ft (27.4m) in height. The original entrance was on the south side, on the first floor, being reached, as usual in Norman castles, by an external stone staircase which has entirely disappeared. The present timber staircase is modern, and approaches the original entrance from the opposite direction. The interior is of the plainest and sternest character. Every consideration is subservient to that of obtaining the greatest strength and security. The outer walls vary in thickness from 15ft (4.6m) in the lower to 11ft (3.3m) in the upper storey. The whole building is crossed from north to south by one wall, which rises from base to summit and divides it into a larger western and a smaller eastern portion. The eastern part is further subdivided by a wall which cuts off the Chapel of St John, its Crypt, and its Sub-crypt, the floors between which are of stone. There is a wooden floor between each of the storeys of the other part.

During the Middle Ages the Keep was truly the White Tower; thus in 1241 Henry III had the royal apartments in the Keep whitewashed, as well as the whole exterior. In addition he had the Chapel of St John decorated with painting and stained glass.

During the wars with France, David, King of Scots, John, King of France, Charles of Blois, and John de Vienne, governor of Calais, and his twelve brave burgesses and many other illustrious prisoners were lodged here. In the Tower Richard II signed his abdication in 1399. The Duke of Orléans, taken at Agincourt, was lodged by Henry V in the White Tower. From that time the Beauchamp and other Towers were more used as prisons, but probably some of the Kentish rebels, taken with Wyat in 1554, slept in the recesses of the Sub-crypt of the Chapel. In 1663 and later years down to 1709, structural repairs were carried out under the superintendence of Sir Christopher Wren, who replaced nearly all the Norman window openings with others of a classical character.

Near a staircase which has now disappeared, on the south side, some children's bones were found in the reign of Charles II. They were identified, with some degree of certainty, with the remains of Edward V and his brother who disappeared so mysteriously at the accession of Richard III.

THE ARMOURIES

There has always been armour in the Tower of London. The present collection took its shape in the reign of Henry VIII, to whose personal interest in the subject many of the present exhibits are due.

At that time the King's armour was distributed between the Tower and Greenwich, Westminster, Hampton Court and Windsor Castle. After the Restoration in 1660, when armour had fallen into disuse, Charles II had it concentrated at the Tower and at Windsor, and so, with few essential changes, it has remained. But the Tower Armouries had been a show place long before 1660 and can claim to be the oldest museum in England. One of the earliest visitors to record his impression was the German traveller Hentzner, and many of the items he saw in 1598 remain on show today. It was in Charles II's time that the historical Line of Kings was first set up, and this feature of the Armouries continued until well into the last century, despite many anachronisms.

At various times additions have been made, and continue to be made, to the Armouries, increasing their scope as the national museum of European arms and armour. But the old Royal nucleus remains, and gives the Armouries a special character; it binds them closely with the history of England.

The body armour worn in the early Middle Ages was chiefly of mail and consisted of a shirt and leggings constructed of riveted, interlinked iron rings; the head was protected by a helmet and a shield was carried on the left arm. This was the accoutrement of William the Conqueror at Hastings, and Richard I and his Crusaders in Palestine. Their weapons were the lance and sword, and, to a lesser degree, the mace and axe. But mail, for all its flexibility, had certain disadvantages, and men began to reinforce it with pieces of plate. This process advanced rapidly during the fourteenth century, and the men-at-arms at Crécy and Poitiers wore a mixture of plate and mail. The advantages of plate armour lay in its glancing surface (like modern streamlining) and its resistance to a direct blow. The full harness of plate from head to foot, or 'white armour' as it was called, was finally evolved at the beginning of the fifteenth century, about the time of Agincourt. The best armour was made in Milan and in South Germany.

The introduction of gunpowder in the fourteenth century at first had little effect, except for siege purposes, and the musket did not finally oust the bow until the sixteenth century. Armour could be made thick enough to

Henry VIII, whose personal armours are displayed in the White Tower

The Royal Armour Gallery in the White Tower, showing armour of Henry VIII and the restored ceiling timbers. The massive cross wall is part of the original structure

resist a bullet, but this greatly increased its weight. Thus in the better organised armies of the sixteenth century, when freer tactical manoeuvring became possible, the heavily armoured horseman found himself at a disadvantage. But the knightly exercise of tilting still kept the armourers busy, and some of the finest craftsmen exercised their skill during this period.

When the English Civil War broke out in 1642 the day of defensive armour was almost over. For a time pikemen still continued to wear half-armour, and the cavalry a helmet and a breast and back plate or a coat of buff leather. Thereafter for nearly two centuries the weapon of offence was supreme, and regiments of the standing army were equipped in distinctive

Opposite page. Top left: Close helmet of William Somerset, 3rd Earl of Worcester, made in the Royal Workshops at Greenwich, c.1570–80. Top right: Close helmet of 'Lion' armour, c.1550. Centre left: Armour with finely etched decoration. South German, c.1550

24

Centre right: Visored bascinet with mail aventail, Milanese, c.1360.
Right: Grotesque helmet presented to Henry VIII by Emperor Maximilian I

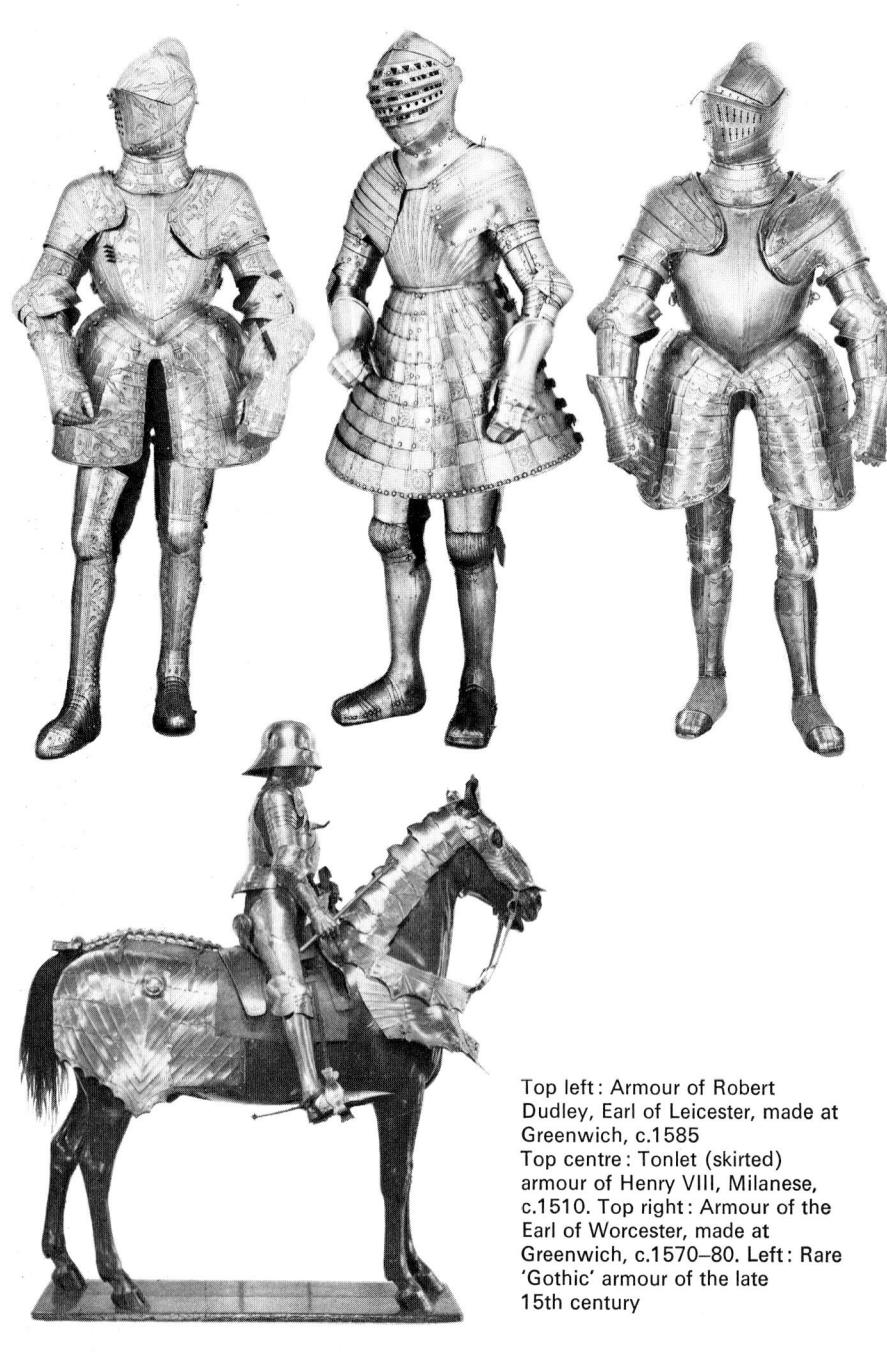

Top left: Armour of Robert Dudley, Earl of Leicester, made at Greenwich, c.1585
Top centre: Tonlet (skirted) armour of Henry VIII, Milanese, c.1510. Top right: Armour of the Earl of Worcester, made at Greenwich, c.1570–80. Left: Rare 'Gothic' armour of the late 15th century

Above: Armour of Henry VIII made at Greenwich in 1540
Top right: German tilt-armour, c.1590, with lance
Right: Armour of Henry VIII for horse and man

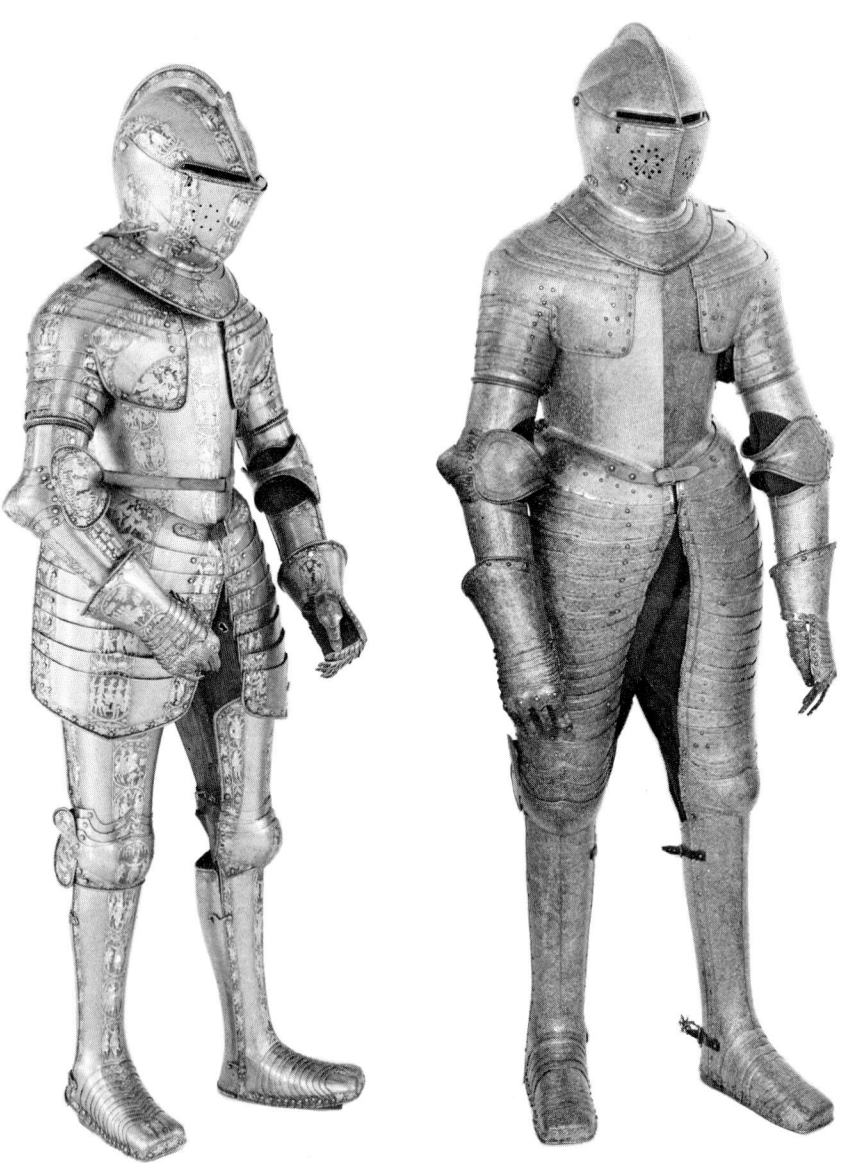

Armour of a Stuart prince, probably Charles II when Prince of Wales, aged about fourteen years. English or French c.1640

Armour of Charles I entirely engraved with flowers and scroll foliage and gilt. Probably English c.1640

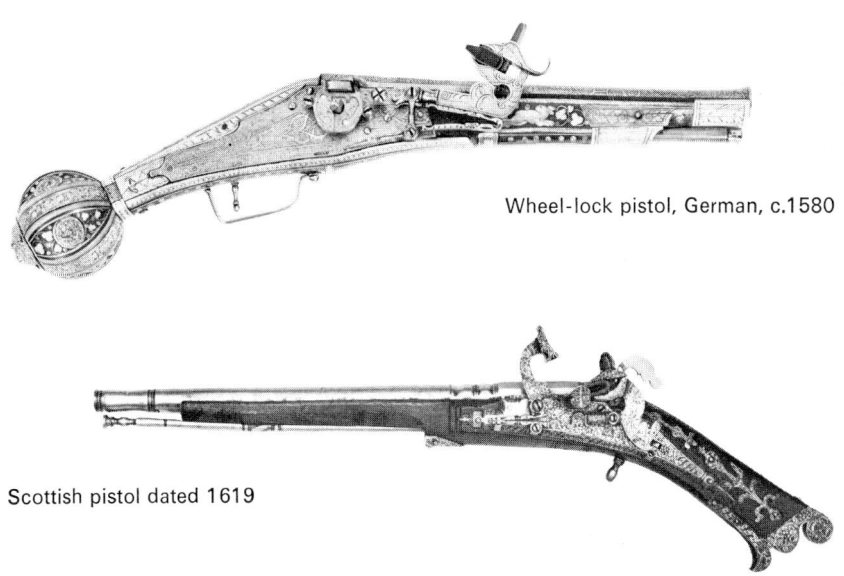

Wheel-lock pistol, German, c.1580

Scottish pistol dated 1619

uniforms of cloth. In our own day armour has returned in the form of the tank, but with the difference that it is mechanically propelled and encases several men instead of one.

Very little armour has survived from a time earlier than the fifteenth century. Mail was particularly liable to deterioration and was often cut up for other uses. Enriched armour of the sixteenth century usually owes its survival to intrinsic merit or personal association; this fact is exemplified in the Tower Armouries by the presence of four armours of Henry VIII and of several of the Elizabethan courtiers and the Stuart princes. The armour of the common soldier had less chance of survival: as a rule it is found only in arsenals whence numbers of retainers were equipped. It is represented in the Armouries by a few jacks and by troopers' and pikemen's armour of the seventeenth century.

Weapons of offence fall into four categories:

1 the *arme blanche*, that is to say, the sword and dagger;
2 arms of percussion : the club, the mace, and the hammer;
3 staff weapons : the lance, spear, pike and axe, and their relatives, the bill, halberd, partisan, etc;
4 projectile weapons, which include *a.* the long bow, crossbow, javelin and sling; *b.* firearms, *e.g.* the cannon and its diminutives, the hand gun (from which developed the musket and later the rifle) and the pistol.

It is worthy of remark that three modern principles in firearms were understood early, namely, breech-loading, the rifled barrel and the revolving chamber, all of which can be seen in the Armouries in weapons dating from the sixteenth and seventeenth centuries.

THE ARRANGEMENT OF THE ARMOURIES

In recent years the display has been rearranged and recased. This is a large task which is only now approaching completion, and it is possible that some galleries in the White Tower will be closed at the time of your visit.

On entering the White Tower the visitor finds himself on the first floor of the building, which now contains the Sporting and Tournament Galleries. The second floor is devoted to European arms and armour from the early Middle Ages to the close of the sixteenth century. The top floor contains armour and weapons from Henry VIII's personal arsenal, Greenwich armours of the sixteenth century, and arms and armour of the seventeenth century.

The Sporting Gallery
This contains weapons which have been used for sport from the Middle Ages to the end of the nineteenth century. There is a fine selection of crossbows, for the hunt and for target shooting, elegant silver mounted hunting swords and a great variety of firearms, from massive elephant guns to richly decorated fowling pieces.

The Tournament Gallery
Here are displayed the different types of armour developed for the joust and for the tournament in the fifteenth and sixteenth centuries. A notable treasure is the late fifteenth century armour for the *Scharfrennen*, a form of joust using sharp lances. There is also a remarkable saddle used in another type of joust, the *Hohenzeuggestech*, in which the contestant stood in his stirrups. Fine decoration is found on foot-combat armour made in 1591 by Anton Peffenhauser for Christian I of Saxony and there are two foot-combat armours for small boys.

The Crypt of St John's Chapel
This contains several inscriptions carved by prisoners who took part in Wyatt's rebellion in 1554. Here are shown the wooden heads and two of the wooden horses carved for the Line of Kings in the 1680s. The Line was the centrepiece of the Armouries display until the late nineteenth century.

St John's Chapel in the White Tower, c.1080

The heads and horses are by Grinling Gibbons and other notable sculptors of the period.

Leaving the crypt the visitor re-enters the Sporting Gallery and ascends by the staircase at the south east angle to the second floor of the Tower, passing through the west doorway of

The Chapel of St John

This chapel rises through two floors of the White Tower and is of the greatest interest because of its survival from an early date, about 1080, unaltered. It is 55ft 6in (16.9m) long and 31ft (9.4m) wide and has a sanctuary and a nave structurally undivided and opening through Romanesque archways to a continuous ambulatory and flanking aisles. The great cylindrical columns of the arcading have simply-carved capitals and carry plain round archways. Above the latter are plain archways to a continuous gallery, known as a tribune, lit by a number of windows in the back wall. The only old fittings in the chapel are the panels of stained glass in the lower windows which came from Horace Walpole's collection at Strawberry Hill. A notice on the north wall lists some of the historic happenings in this chapel. Leaving the chapel by the north doorway the visitor enters

The Medieval Gallery

Here are displayed arms and armour from the Classical period to the close of the fifteenth century. There is a wide range of medieval swords, including a great processional sword of the fifteenth century. Here too are important examples of early plate armour. The visored bascinet, with its original aventail (protecting the neck), dates from the late fourteenth century and is from the famous armoury at Churburg Castle. The German armour for man and horse is of great rarity. Scale models and illustrations are used

The execution block and axe

Above: Medieval swords of the 10th to the 15th centuries

Below: Rapiers of the 16th and 17th centuries

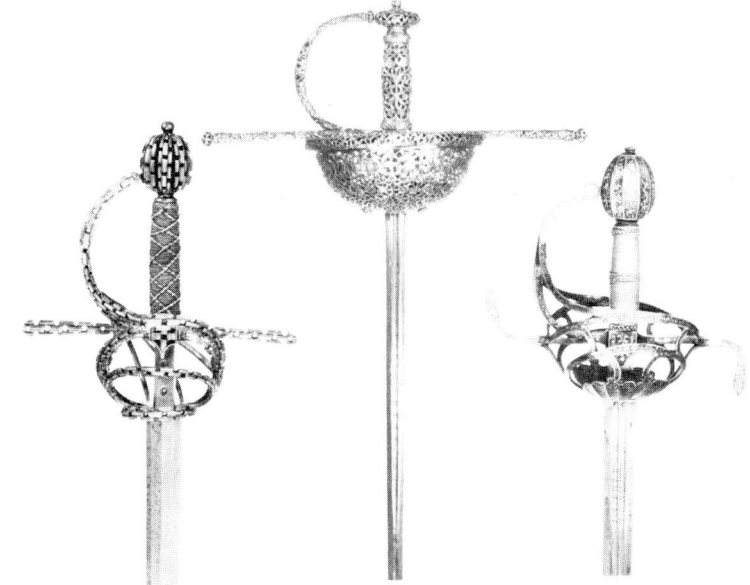

to demonstrate the evolution of medieval armour. Infantry arms are represented by staff weapons, and there are several painted pavises (shields).

The Sixteenth Century Gallery
This room contains several fine armours, including a very richly decorated parade harness known as the 'Lion' armour, which was probably made in France about 1540, and the 'giant' armour for a man about 6ft 10in (2.08m) in height. A splendid bright steel armour, made in the Royal workshops at Greenwich about 1580, was long used in the Line of Kings for the figure of William the Conqueror! Other cases show the equipment of ordinary soldiers, including two longbow staves found in the wreck of the *Mary Rose*, sunk in 1545, which are almost the only surviving examples of England's national weapon. Another display features finely decorated firearms.

Ascending the stairs at the north-west angle, facing the parade ground, the visitors enter

The Royal Armour Gallery
This was originally the Council Chamber and has witnessed many memorable scenes in the medieval history of this country, including Richard III's denunciation of Lord Hastings, who was summarily executed outside. It now houses four of the personal armours of Henry VIII, together with weapons from his arsenal and a number of fine personal armours of leading courtiers which were made in the Royal Workshops at Greenwich during the second half of the sixteenth century. The Greenwich workshops were established by Henry VIII, and the King's foot combat harness is one of their earliest works. The skirted, or 'tonlet', armour was also made for the young king, so too was the fine armour for man and horse, the whole surface of which is engraved and was originally silvered. Henry's later obesity can be judged from the massive garniture (armour with interchangeable pieces for tournament and field use) made at Greenwich in 1540. Note also the helmet with ram's horns, given to Henry by the Emperor Maximilian I. The weapons from the King's arsenal include a unique series of gun shields, a spiked club with three pistol barrels in the head, known as 'Henry VIII's Walking Staff', an enormous lance reputedly that of Charles Brandon, Duke of Suffolk, the King's boon companion, and many spears, bills and partisans carried by members of the Royal Guard.

The later Greenwich armours include that made for Robert Dudley, Earl of Leicester (embossed with his badge of a bear and ragged staff), and those for other prominent members of Queen Elizabeth's court.

The Seventeenth Century Gallery
This room includes the Stuart Royal armours, including the gilt harness of Charles I and a richly decorated armour made for Charles II when Prince of Wales. In the case opposite them is the buff coat traditionally worn by Colonel Hacker, who officiated at the execution of Charles I in Whitehall in 1649. Equipment for cavalry and infantry forces is displayed, and there is a

The Tower of London from across the River Thames

Yeoman Warders on Ceremonial Church Parade

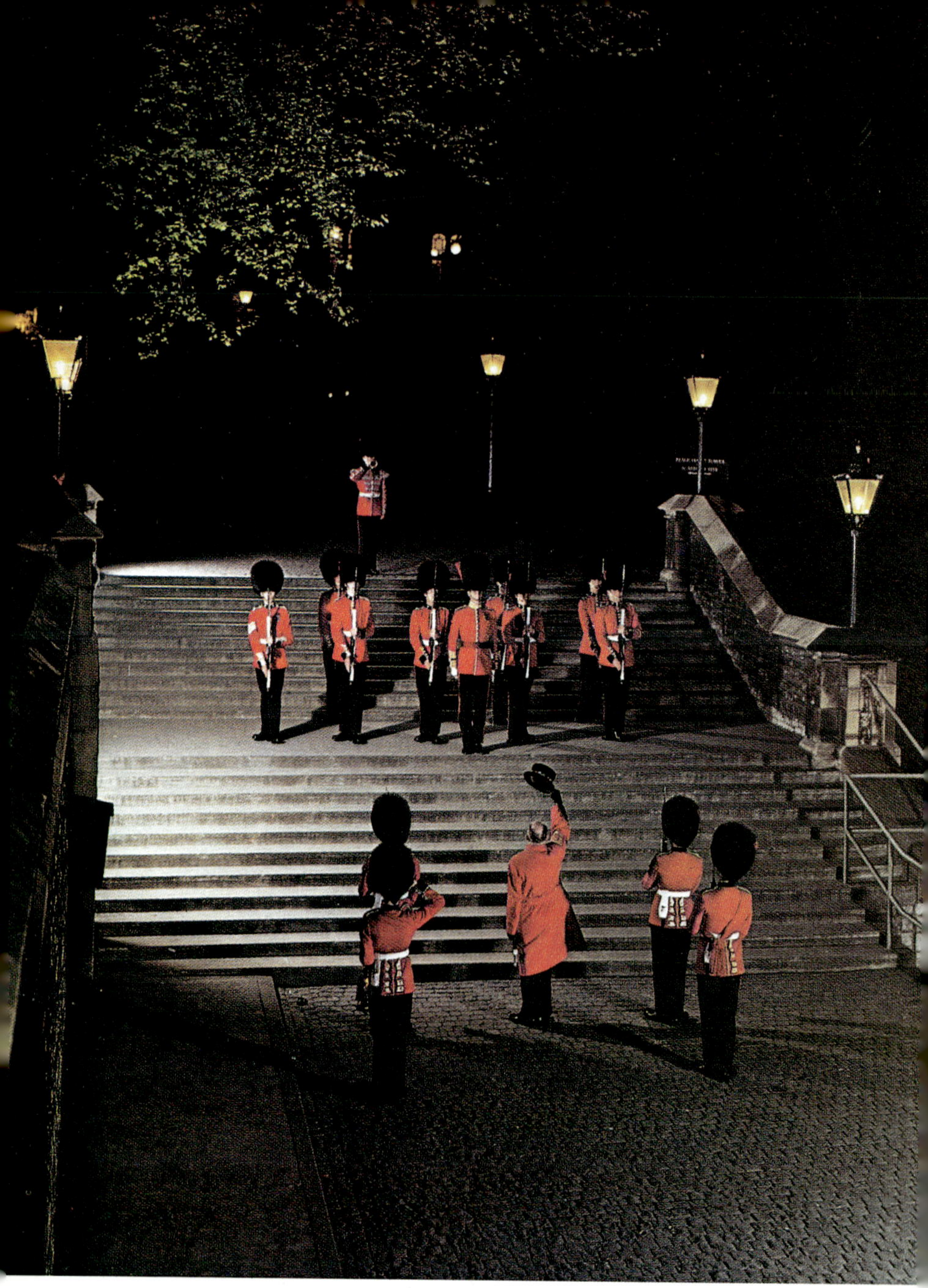

case of richly decorated rapiers and firearms. The visitor leaves this gallery by the north stairway and descends to the basement.

It was in the basement that the rack was installed in the sixteenth century and many prisoners were brought to these vaults for examination. The original wooden ceiling was replaced by the present brick vaults about 1720 and the area converted into an arms store. The present display recreates the atmosphere of this eighteenth-century arsenal.

The visitor first enters

The Mortar Room

Here are shown bronze mortars, with other pieces of ordnance. In the centre bay room is a large mortar used at the siege of Namur in 1695, which is said to have been fired so frequently that the touch hole or vent became fused with heat. The original timber carriage was burnt in the Tower fire of 1841, which destroyed the Grand Storehouse; it has recently been restored.

At the far end is a mortar of nine bores used for fireworks at the peace of Aix-la-Chapelle in 1748. On the walls are helmets, cuirasses, muskets, rifles, and wall pieces together with military swords and lances; the helmets and cuirasses were captured from the French during the Napoleonic wars. The carved stone panel of the Lion of St Mark was brought from Corfu in 1809.

At the south end of the Mortar Room is the sub-crypt of the Chapel of St John, which has a barrel vault and was dimly lit from the east. This may have been occasionally used for keeping prisoners, but was normally a storeroom. It now contains finely decorated small cannon of the sixteenth and seventeenth centuries and a gilded wooden lion, also brought from Corfu.

In the west wall is an opening cut in the eighteenth century, when the basement was used as a powder store. It gives access to

The Cannon Room

Here are several guns brought up from the seabed, including one dredged from the wreck of the *Mary Rose*, sunk in 1545. There are also bronze guns made for Henry VIII, including an unusual three-barrelled breech-loading cannon, with other examples of English and foreign guns. On the walls are various staff weapons of the sixteenth and seventeenth centuries, including long pikes, halberds, and bills. The well on the east side dates from the twelfth century and is 40ft (12m) deep. When it was cleaned out in 1910 the wooden frame on which its stones were built was found in place at the bottom.

With this room the tour of the White Tower is completed.

The Ceremony of the Keys

The Royal Chapel of St Peter ad Vincula: early 16th century

THE BROAD WALK

This is the open space between the Waterloo Block (formerly Barracks) on the north and the White Tower on the south. The Barracks were built in 1845 on the site of the Great Storehouse burnt in 1841. The building of similar character to the right contains the Regimental Headquarters and Museum of the Royal Fusiliers (City of London Regiment).

THE WATERLOO BLOCK

The ground floor houses the Oriental Gallery, with a spectacular display of eastern arms and armour. The famous eighteenth-century elephant armour was brought from India by Lord Clive. The first floor of the building now houses the Education Centre, which has extensive facilities for school parties and other organised groups.

THE BOWYER TOWER

This thirteenth-century tower now houses a small collection of instruments of torture and punishment, including the block and axe.

THE ROYAL FUSILIERS MUSEUM

This contains relics and trophies dating from the formation of the regiment in 1685 to the present day and a fine display of silver and china. Uniforms include those worn by George V as Colonel-in-Chief, and the collection of medals contains three Victoria Crosses. Dioramas depict the battles of Albuera (1811), Alma (1854), Mons (1914), and Cassino (1944), in which the Royal Fusiliers played a distinguished part.

THE NEW ARMOURIES

This red brick building was constructed as a storehouse for the Board of Ordnance in the third quarter of the seventeenth century. It now houses the offices of the Armouries and a gallery devoted to the history of the Board of Ordnance, which was until 1855, the government department responsible for the supply of all arms to the British army and navy.

THE CHAPEL ROYAL OF ST PETER AD VINCULA

This is so called from having been consecrated on that well-known festival of the Latin Church, August 1st, probably in the reign of Henry I (1100–35). The chapel was rebuilt at the end of the thirteenth century. It was burnt in 1512 and almost entirely rebuilt, and has since then undergone a great deal of repair. (*Guided parties are admitted only under a Yeoman Warder.*) In the memorable words of Stow, writing in the reign of Queen Elizabeth I, there lie before the high altar 'two dukes between two queens, to wit, the Duke of Somerset and the Duke of Northumberland, between Queen Anne and Queen Katharine, all four beheaded'. Here also are buried Lady Jane Grey and Lord Guildford Dudley, the Duke of Monmouth, and the Scottish lords, Kilmarnock, Balmerino, and Lovat, beheaded for their share in the rebellion of 1745. The last burial in the chapel was that of Charles Wyndham, Keeper of the Regalia, in 1872; the canopied tomb of John Holland, Duke of Exeter and Constable of the Tower, who died in 1447, was brought here in 1951, having been previously moved from its original position in St Katharine's Hospital by the Tower in 1827.

TOWER GREEN

The space south of the chapel is so called, and was used as a burial ground; in the middle is a small square plot paved with granite, showing the site on which stood at rare intervals the scaffold for private executions. It was paved by order of Queen Victoria. The following persons are known to have been executed on or near this spot:

1   William, Lord Hastings, by order of Richard, Duke of Gloucester, in June 1483.
2   Queen Anne Boleyn, second wife of Henry VIII, 19 May 1536.
3   Margaret, Countess of Salisbury, the last of the old Angevin or Plantagenet family, 27 May 1541.
4   Queen Katharine Howard, fifth wife of Henry VIII, 13 February 1542.
5   Jane, Viscountess Rochford, 13 February 1542.
6   Lady Jane Grey, wife of Lord Guildford Dudley, 12 February 1554.
7   Robert Devereux, Earl of Essex, 25 February 1601.

They were all beheaded with an axe except Queen Anne Boleyn, whose head was cut off with a sword by an executioner brought over from St Omer. The bodies of all seven were buried in the Chapel of St Peter.

THE BEAUCHAMP TOWER

This is on the west side of Tower Green, facing the White Tower, and is on the inner wall between the Bell Tower on the south and the Devereux Tower on the north, being connected with both by a walk along the wall-top. Its present name probably refers to the residence in it, as a prisoner, of Thomas, third Earl of Warwick, of the Beauchamp family, who was

Part of a mural painting of the 14th century, discovered in the Byward Tower in 1953

attainted under Richard II in 1397, but restored to his honours and liberty two years later under Henry IV. It is curious that the most interesting associations of the place should be with his successors in the earldom. Although built entirely for defensive purposes, we find it thus early used as a prison, and during the two following centuries it seems to have been regarded as one of the most convenient places in which to lodge prisoners of rank; in consequence many of the most interesting mural inscriptions are to be found in its chambers.

In plan the Beauchamp Tower is semicircular, and it projects 18ft (5.5m) beyond the face of the wall. It consists of three storeys, of which the middle one is on a level with the rampart, on which it formerly opened. The building dates from the reign of Edward I, though on the line of Richard I's defences; the brickwork is of the time of Henry VIII. It is entered at the south-east corner and a circular staircase ascends to the middle chamber, which is spacious and has a large window and a fireplace. Here are to be found most of the inscriptions, some having been brought from other chambers. A few are in the entrance passage and on the stairs. All are numbered and catalogued. The following – to which the numbers are appended – will be found the most interesting.

On the ground floor, near the entrance, ROBART DVDLEY (2). This was the fifth son of John, Duke of Northumberland, and next brother to Guildford Dudley, the husband of Lady Jane Grey. When his father was brought to the block in 1553 he and his brother remained in prison here, Guildford being condemned to death in 1554. In the following year he was liberated with his

Prisoners' inscriptions on the walls of Beauchamp Tower
Left: G Gifford, 1586. Centre: The Dudley brothers, 1553
Right: T Salmon, 1622

The Queen's House on Tower Green

elder brother, Ambrose, afterwards created Earl of Warwick, and his younger brother, Henry. In the first year of Queen Elizabeth I he was made Master of the Horse and chosen a Knight of the Garter. In 1564 he was created Earl of Leicester. He died at Cornbury, in Oxfordshire, in 1588.

On the left, at the entrance of the great chamber, is a carved cross, with other religious emblems, with the name and arms of PEVEREL, and the date 1570 (8). It is supposed to have been cut by a Roman Catholic prisoner confined in the reign of Elizabeth I.

Over the fireplace this inscription in Latin: 'The more suffering for Christ in this world the more glory with Christ in the next', etc (13). This is signed 'Arundel, June 22, 1587'. This was Philip Howard, son of Thomas, Duke of Norfolk, beheaded in 1572. Philip inherited from his maternal grandfather the Earldom of Arundel in 1580. He was a staunch Roman Catholic and was constantly under suspicion of the Government, by which in 1584 he was confined in his own house for a short time. On his liberation he determined to quit the country, but was committed to the Tower in 1585, and died in custody ten years later, having refused release on condition of forsaking his religion. His body was buried in his father's grave in the Chapel of St Peter, but was eventually removed to Arundel. He left other inscriptions, one in the window (79), and one on the staircase (91), dated 1587.

On the right of the fireplace is an elaborate piece of sculpture (14), which will be examined with peculiar interest as a memorial of the five brothers Dudley: Ambrose (created Earl of Warwick 1561), Guildford (beheaded 1554), Robert (created Earl of Leicester 1546), and Henry (killed at the siege of St Quentin. 1557), carved by the eldest, John (called Earl of Warwick), who died in 1554. Under a bear and a lion supporting a ragged staff is the name of 'JOHN DVDLE' and surrounding them is a wreath of roses (for Ambrose), oak leaves (for Robert, *robur*, an oak), gillyflowers (for Guildford), and honeysuckle (for Henry). Below are four lines, one of them incomplete, alluding to the device and its meaning. It is on record that the Lieutenant of the Tower was allowed 6s 8d a day each for the diet of these captive brothers.

No. 33 is one of several inscriptions relating to the Poole or Pole family. (*See also* Nos. 45, 47, 52, 56, 57.) They were the grandsons of the Countess of Salisbury, who was beheaded in 1541. No. 45 contains the name of 'GEFFRYE POOLE 1562'. He was the second son, and he gave evidence against his elder brother, Lord Montagu, who was beheaded in 1539.

'IANE' (48). This interesting inscription, repeated also in the window (85), has always been supposed to refer to Lady Jane Grey, daughter of the Duke of Suffolk and wife of Guildford Dudley, fourth son of the Duke of Northumberland. A second repetition in another part of the room was unfortunately obliterated in the last century when a new window was made to fit this chamber for a mess-room. It is sometimes, but erroneously, supposed that the name was carved by this Queen of ten days herself, but it is improbable that she was ever imprisoned in the Beauchamp Tower. She is known to have lived in the house of Partridge, the Gaoler. It is much more probable that the two inscriptions were placed on the wall either by Lord Guildford Dudley, her husband, or by her brother, whose large device has been described above (14).

In the window is the rebus, or monogram, of Thomas Abell (66); upon a bell is the letter A. This was Dr Abell, a faithful servant to Queen Katharine of Aragon, first wife of Henry VIII. He acted as her chaplain during the progress of the divorce, and by his determined advocacy offended the King. For denying Royal supremacy in the Church he was condemned and executed in 1540. There are many other records of this kind in the Beauchamp Tower.

On leaving Beauchamp Tower and turning to the right the visitor sees, facing Tower Green,

THE QUEEN'S HOUSE

Until about 1880 this was called The Lieutenant's Lodgings. The present

Some famous Tower prisoners

Left and right:

Queen Anne Boleyn
1507–1536
Judge Jeffreys
1648–1689

Robert Dudley,
Earl of Leicester
1532–1588
Queen Elizabeth I
1533–1603

Sir Walter Ralegh
1552–1618
Painting thought
to be Margaret,
Countess of Salisbury
1473–1541

Left and right:

Robert Devereux,
Earl of Essex
1566–1601
Simon Frazer,
Lord Lovat
1667–1747

Sir Thomas More
1478–1535
James, Duke of
Monmouth
1649–1685

Lord Nithsdale
1676–1744
Thomas Cromwell,
Earl of Essex
1485–1540

house was built in about 1530 and may have replaced the medieval constable's house. It is a good example of a timber-framed house and originally contained a spacious hall two storeys in height. A floor was later inserted in the upper part of the hall and the resultant room became known as the Council Chamber. It contains an elaborate contemporary memorial tablet of the Gunpowder Plot – it was in this room that the interrogation of the conspirators took place. In the north wing is the small room where Anne Boleyn spent the last days of her life. On the west side is the rampart known as Elizabeth's Walk. The front door may be that through which in 1716 Lord Nithsdale escaped in female attire the evening before he was to have been beheaded. As a result of the ill-starred Stuart rebellion of 1715, Nithsdale and six other Scottish nobles were brought up to London and paraded through the streets to prison. They were tried in February, 1716, and condemned to death. Three were later pardoned. Nithsdale's young wife had braved snowbound roads all the way from their home in Dumfriesshire to plead for his life. When that failed, she persuaded a woman friend to put on two dresses and go with her to the condemned cell – where Nithsdale donned the spare dress and made good his escape, eventually travelling to Rome disguised, this time as one of the footmen of the Venetian Ambassador.

The interior of the Queen's House is not shown to the public. Next to it stood the house where Lady Jane Grey lived when a prisoner, and from its windows saw her husband go forth from the adjoining Beauchamp Tower to his execution on Tower Hill and his headless body brought to the Chapel 'in a carre', while on the green in front, the scaffold was being prepared for her own execution on the same day, Monday, 12th February, 1554.

THE SALT TOWER

This was formerly called Julius Caesar's Tower and is of special interest as containing more prisoners' inscriptions than any other, except the Beauchamp Tower; they are, moreover, in their original places, while many of those in the Beauchamp Tower are not. Among them the most conspicuous is the figure for casting horoscopes cut by Hew Draper of Bristol in 1561. He was sent to the Tower for an accusation of witchcraft against Lady St Lo, better known as Bess of Hardwick, and her husband Sir William St Lo. A finely cut armillary sphere is also to be seen, and a pierced heart, hand and foot occur in different places on the wall, signifying the five wounds of Christ. The name of Michael Moody, 1587, recalls a plot to murder Elizabeth I, and here as in the other tower are several inscriptions marked by the IHS monogram, with a cross above the H, a form commonly used by members of the Society of Jesus.

THE MARTIN TOWER

This is of Henry III's time though it has been much cut about and modernised. It had originally a single room on each floor, and remains of embrasures and the large stone fireplaces are to be seen. There are a number prisoners' inscriptions, mostly of the early seventeenth century, about the time of the Gunpowder Plot. This tower was formerly inhabited by the Keeper of the Regalia, and was the scene of the attempt by Colonel Blood in 1671 to steal the State Crown and other regalia. Having first spied out the land in clerical disguise, and ingratiated himself with the old keeper, Talbot Edwards, Blood came back with two accomplices, all being armed with pistols, swordsticks and daggers. Leaving poor Edwards for dead (in fact, he died a few years afterwards), Blood hid the Crown under his cloak, while one companion put the Orb in his breeches pocket, and the other started filing the Sceptre in half to carry away. At this point they were disturbed by Edwards' son; and in the running fight that followed, Blood and his companions were captured.

Blood's enigmatic remark that 'it was a brave attempt, for it was for a crown', coupled with the fact that Charles II not only pardoned him forthwith, but conferred a pension and certain Irish estates on him, led some to suppose either that Charles, in need of money, had commissioned Blood to steal the treasures, or that Blood knew some awkward secrets about the King.

The Martin Tower was damaged by bomb-blast in the last war.

BASTION OF THE ROMAN LONDON WALL

The remains of the medieval Wardrobe Tower incorporate the base of a Roman tower of U-shaped plan and apparently hollow. This base of rubble masonry with a double bonding course of tiles set in pink mortar stands to a height of 5ft (1.5m). The large-gritted buff mortar of the Roman rubble work is quite distinct from the whitish mortar of the medieval reconstruction. There is also a 10ft (3m) length of wall standing to a height of nearly 5ft (1.5m) at the back of the Wardrobe Tower. The line of this fragment, if produced southwards, would strike the Lanthorn Tower (*see plan*).

NORTH FRONT

On the outer circuit of wall at the north-west and north-east angles are two bastions added by Henry VIII, known as Legge's Mount and Brass Mount respectively. There was a similar bastion at the north angle, added in the reign of Queen Victoria at the time of the Chartist riots – the last addition to the fortifications of the Tower. Its destruction by a German bomb on 5th October, 1940, revealed the original line of the Curtain Wall, which has now been rebuilt instead of the bastion. Two other buildings of the Tower were destroyed by enemy bombs, the modern Main Guard between the Wakefield and White Towers (29th December, 1940 – *see page* 13), and the north end of the late eighteenth-century 'Hospital Block', to the east of the White Tower (22nd September, 1940), now rebuilt.

RIVER FRONT AND WHARF

East of St Thomas's Tower two further towers should be noted on the outer curtain. The Cradle Tower is a fourteenth-century water-gate with a contemporary vault similar to that in the gate-passage beneath the Bloody Tower, but the present upper part of the tower dates from the nineteenth century. Further to the east and beyond a modern entrance through the curtain, the Well Tower also has an original vault of the time of Henry III.

The Wharf itself in its present form is relatively recent, but evidence for a wharf at the Tower of London goes back to the early fourteenth century, and by the end of that century a stone wharf stretched along practically the whole of the river frontage of the Tower.

Here may be seen a number of guns of historic interest from many parts of the world.

Among the large guns which may be seen on the Wharf or River Front are two richly decorated bronze guns cast in 1762 from ordnance taken at Cherbourg, a battery of French field guns captured at Waterloo, a saluting battery of three carronades, a line of English 32 and 64 pdr. garrison or naval guns, and mortars from Corfu presented by the Ionian Government in 1842.

Between the outer and inner walls on the river side is a line of iron guns including Russian guns from the Crimea, two guns of Sussex iron made by John Fuller in 1747, and a gun from HMS *Royal George*. In various positions around the White Tower are a battery of English mortars from the Crimea, the famous 'Dardanelles' gun cast in 1464 for the Sultan Mahomed II and presented to Queen Victoria in 1867, a large Turkish gun made in 1530 and captured at Aden in 1839, and the long Flemish gun on its 'Maltese' carriage, which is a delightful extravaganza.

TRADITION OF THE TOWER

Among events of tradition and pageantry that take place at the Tower the following should be mentioned.

Firing a Royal Salute

ROYAL SALUTES

The Governor of the Tower has the duty of giving notice in writing to the Honourable Artillery Company that a Royal Salute is due to be fired from the Tower on a particular day. For a great State event the proper salute is 62 guns; likewise for the anniversary of the Sovereign's birth, accession, or coronation. When Parliament is opened by the Sovereign in person the appropriate salute is 41 guns; it is the same for the birth of a Royal infant. A troop of four guns of the Honourable Artillery Company fires the salute from the Gun Park at the west end of the wharf.

THE CEREMONY OF THE KEYS

A ceremony centuries old is enacted every night at 10 p.m. when the main gates of the Tower are locked. Five minutes before the hour the Chief Yeoman Warder joins an escort consisting of a sergeant and three men who

Yeoman Warders in ceremonial dress

are detailed to help him close the three gates. When the keys return, the sentry calls a challenge: 'Halt, who goes there?' The Chief Warder replies: 'The keys.' The exchange continues with 'Whose keys?' – 'Queen Elizabeth's keys.' Keys and escort then proceed through the Bloody Tower arch, where they encounter the whole Guard formed up on the steps leading to the Broad Walk. Then the guard present arms: the Chief Warder, doffing his Tudor bonnet, calls: 'God preserve Queen Elizabeth'; and the whole guard respond: 'Amen.' The keys are finally carried by the Chief Warder to the Queen's House where they are secured for the night.

BEATING THE BOUNDS

In Anglo-Saxon times it was the boys who were beaten at parish boundaries so that they were made sure of remembering them; nowadays the boys give instead of receiving a beating. Every third year at Rogationtide the bounds of the Tower Liberty are beaten by residents and children dwelling within the Tower, assisted by choirboys from neighbouring parishes. After a service in St Peter ad Vincula a procession is formed by the Governor, Chaplain, Warders, residents, and choir, the children carrying white wands.

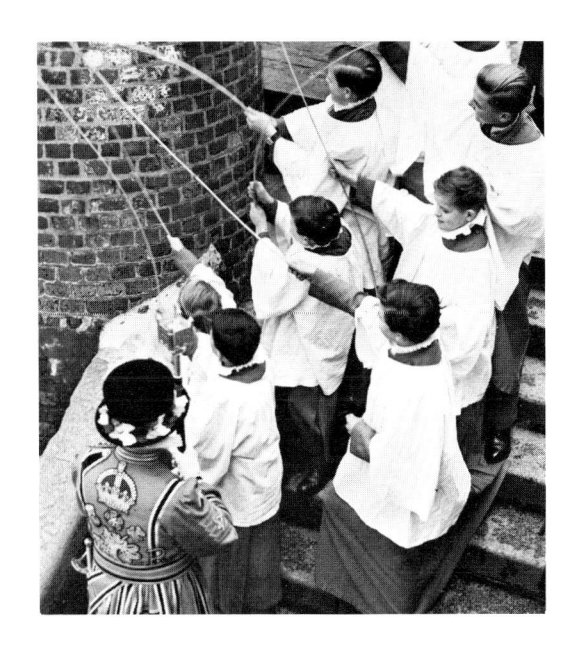

Choirboys of St Peter ad Vincula beating the bounds

There are 31 boundary stones, and at each of them the Chaplain proclaims: 'Cursed is he that removeth his neighbours' landmark', and the Chief Warder urges the beaters on with: 'Whack it, boys, whack it.'

INSTALLATION OF THE CONSTABLE

The office of Constable of the Tower has existed almost since the Norman Conquest, for William I made the first appointment about 1078 to reward Geoffrey de Mandeville for good service at the Battle of Hastings and elsewhere. Always regarded as an office of honour and dignity – in the Middle Ages, of profit also – it is held by Royal Letters Patent under the Great Seal and confers the privilege of audience and direct communication with the Sovereign. In 1933 the tenure was altered from life to five years. A long line of distinguished prelates, soldiers, and statesmen who have been Constable includes William Longchamp, Bishop of Ely; Walter de Stapleton, Bishop of Exeter; the Duke of Wellington, from 1826 to 1852 (since when every Constable has been a soldier); Lord Napier of Magdala; Lord Wavell; Lord Alanbrooke; Lord Wilson of Libya; Lord Alexander of Tunis; and since 1975 Field-Marshal Sir Geoffrey Baker.

When a new Constable is installed a traditional ceremony is carried out on Tower Green. The Yeoman Warders, a body appointed by Henry VII, form up in a circle, while a detachment of troops is in attendance. The Lord Chamberlain arrives at the steps near the Bloody Tower and proceeds to the Queen's House, where the keys are handed to him by the Lieutenant of the Tower. The Sovereign's proclamation that the new incumbent shall 'have, hold, exercise, and enjoy' his functions having been read by the Lieutenant, the keys are delivered to the Constable by the Lord Chamberlain, whereupon the Chief Warder cries: 'God preserve Queen Elizabeth', and all the Warders respond: 'Amen.' The new Constable inaugurates his office by carrying out an inspection of the Warders and troops on parade.

THE RAVENS

Ravens were once common in London's streets and were protected for the services they rendered as scavengers. It is probable that there have always been ravens at the Tower, and there is a legend that the Tower will fall if it loses its ravens. The birds are therefore carefully guarded. Six are kept 'on the establishment' and are cared for by a Yeoman Warder who is the Yeoman Ravenmaster.

Each bird receives a weekly ration allowance. They have their own quarters in a cage by the Lanthorn Tower.

Before their wings were clipped ravens have wandered from the Tower, and there was one that used to fly off to perch on St Paul's Cathedral. In the winter of 1889-90 a bird, probably this same one, took up residence in Kensington Gardens.

Ravens can attain a good age and one of the Tower birds, James Crow, was a resident for 44 years. The birds are not popular with everyone; they are often noisy, and will amuse themselves by removing putty from windows, causing damage to unattended cars, and taking sly pecks at ladies' legs!

The ravens on Tower Green

ACKNOWLEDGMENTS

The picture of the Royal Mint on page 14 is from an engraving in the Guildhall Library.

The portrait of Henry VIII on page 23 is from the Tower Armouries.

The portrait of Lord Nithsdale on page 47 is reproduced by courtesy of the Trustees of the Scottish National Portrait Gallery.

All the other portraits on pages 46 and 47 are reproduced by courtesy of the Trustees of the National Portrait Gallery, London.

GENERAL INFORMATION

Photography, Sketching. These are permitted provided no obstruction or nuisance is caused. *No photography whatever is permitted in the Jewel House.*
Guides. Yeoman Warders guide parties round the Tower, leaving the Middle Tower (West Gate) at regular intervals.
Restaurant. Open to the public on days when the Tower is open to visitors from 10 am to 6 pm in summer; from 10 am to 5 pm in winter.
Wharf front. Open, admission free, through East and West Gates. Weekdays: 7 am to sunset. Sundays: 10 am to sunset.

TRANSPORT

Railway. Fenchurch Street Station, 4 minutes' walk. Liverpool Street Station, $\frac{3}{4}$ mile (78 bus). London Bridge Station, $\frac{1}{2}$ mile (47 bus to Tower Bridge Road, then 6 minutes' walk or 42 or 78 bus).
Buses. 42, 78, or any bus crossing Tower Bridge.
Green Line Coaches. Minories Coach Station, $\frac{1}{4}$ mile.
Underground. Tower Hill Station (Inner Circle or District), 2 minutes' walk.

SEASON TICKETS, valid for a year from date of issue, give admission to this and other monuments looked after by the Department of the Environment, Scottish Office or Welsh Office. The tickets can be purchased at many of the monuments, from HMSO Bookshops, or by direct application to any of the above Departments. Family season tickets are also available.

Printed in England for Her Majesty's Stationery Office by
Brown Knight & Truscott Ltd.   Dd 0697723 K 2028/5/80